STACEY ABRAMS
Lift Every Voice

by **Sarah Warren**

illustrated by **Monica Mikai**

Lee & Low Books Inc.
New York

LEE & LOW BOOKS Inc., 95 Madison Avenue, New York, NY 10016

leeandlow.com

Edited by Cheryl Klein

Book design by Christy Hale

Book production by The Kids at Our House

The text is set in Jubilat.

Manufactured in China by RR Donnelley

10 9 8 7 6 5 4 3 2 1

First Edition

Cataloging-in-Publication data is on file
with the Library of Congress.

ISBN 978-1-64379-497-6

*This book is for you, Dad. Thank you for making
the world a better place.* —S.W.

Dedicated to Robert, Alice, and Heather —M.M.

The United States promises that the people can have a voice in deciding who is in charge.

Stacey Abrams makes sure leaders keep that promise.
She helps people understand their power and use it.

VOTE HERE

This work started a long time ago.

Before Stacey was born, her parents were part of the civil rights movement, fighting to make sure Black people everywhere could vote. Growing up, Stacey listened to their stories.

Her parents had three central rules:

Go to church. Go to school. Take care of each other.

They believed all things were possible as long as people looked out for one another. Stacey and her five brothers and sisters were taught to believe that too.

Stacey's dad worked overtime in the shipyard. Still, their family didn't have much. *Having nothing is not an excuse for doing nothing*, he told them. So Stacey served soup from huge pots to hungry neighbors. She learned to ask, *How can I help?*

And Stacey had one treasure nobody could steal: her mind. Stacey loved books. She read her way through encyclopedias, the dictionary, and all kinds of stories.

The law said Stacey had the right to an equal education, but some schools got more support than others. Her parents rented a house as close as they could get to a decent school. Stacey did so well that sometimes a special bus took her to a school with all the books and equipment she would ever need to get ahead.

None of the other kids looked like Stacey.

On election days, Stacey's mom picked the kids up from school. They followed her into a gym graced with voting booths. Stacey loved elections. Voters had power. Her parents chose leaders who would improve life in their city and across the country. Someday, Stacey would have the chance to select her leaders too.

Stacey graduated at the top of her class. She and other Georgia valedictorians were invited to meet the governor. Stacey and her parents took the long bus ride to his mansion. A mansion! Just like the ones on television. They walked up the driveway that stretched to his gate, but the guard wouldn't let her family in. Stacey deserved a spot in that mansion, but her parents had to fight for it.

When Stacey finally got into the party, all she could think about was that guard. He decided who belonged and who didn't. He had the power to open the gate.

Stacey chose to attend Spelman College in Atlanta, a historically Black institution. Stacey had almost never seen other Black people in charge, but at Spelman, she met Black businesspeople, artists, scientists, and scholars.

Outside of class, Stacey attended
city meetings, where she saw how the mayor,
the first Black man to lead Atlanta, looked out for hundreds of
thousands of people. If he could do it, maybe she could too.

Then the world was reminded that Black lives still did not
count like they should.

On the other side of the country, in Los Angeles, California, police officers were caught on camera beating a Black man named Rodney King. A year later, in 1992, a jury decided that the officers didn't do anything wrong. The whole nation witnessed how unfairly Black people were often treated. Some people were surprised. Some were not. Many were angry.

Rage burned through Atlanta.

Many students marched in protest, but stayed out of the violence.

The police came anyway.

Newscasters described the destruction, but ignored the stories of the young people in the streets. Stacey knew Black youth deserved better: Better schools. More opportunity. Equal treatment under the law. If the system were fair, people wouldn't feel the need to rise up.

How could Stacey help? She called the reporters and asked them to tell the whole truth.

No.

She called again.

Click.

She called again.

Nobody would listen.

How would she get them to pay attention? Stacey handed out phone numbers. Classmates called . . . and called . . . and called. News stations demanded to know who was blocking their lines. The students offered one name: Stacey Abrams.

Stacey couldn't change what the media reported, but they asked her to join the conversation. She appeared on television with the mayor. Young Black people were under attack. He should understand their fury. He didn't. Stacey knew the mayor had the power to do more. She told him so.

Young people needed new leaders who cared about their lives. How could Stacey help? She registered other students to vote.

Speaking up was scary, but people were listening. From the steps of the Lincoln Memorial, Stacey told the biggest crowd she had ever seen to give young people the chance to succeed.

The mayor had listened too. He asked Stacey to come work in his office. She had wanted him to look out for the young people of Atlanta. Now she helped him do it.

Stacey graduated from Spelman with top honors, but
she went back to school to study governance and the law.

When she needed a break, she turned
to books. This time, she wrote her own.

As a lawyer in Atlanta, Stacey helped businesses and
the city government follow the rules, especially around
money. Stacey knew how important money was. When she was
growing up, there were times when her family had to go without
electricity or running water. Even as an adult, she didn't always have
enough money to cover her bills and take care of the people she loved.
Like her, many Georgians were not able to buy what they needed to feel
healthy and safe. Better laws could change that. How could she help?

Stacey ran for office and won a seat in the Georgia House of Representatives. She was so good at making laws that she became the leader of her party in the House. Stacey was the first Black woman to hold the job. She had her own way of doing things: She listened. She learned. She agitated and collaborated.

She encouraged other new leaders to run for office too.

Stacey could suggest and vote on laws, but she didn't have the power to decide how those laws worked in people's lives. If she was governor, she'd be able to do more.

Would that be asking for too much? No Black woman had ever won a governor's race in America. If Stacey made people hope that change was possible, how would they feel if she lost? Her fear was big and real. Her need to try was bigger. She decided to run for governor.

In rib shacks, at taquerias, and in packed auditoriums, through videos and postcards and texts, over the phone, and in multiple languages, knocking on door after door, Stacey and her team spread her message:

"We are trying to create a state of excellent schools, with jobs that create wealth and opportunity, with good leaders who stand up for all of us. . . . We are here to ensure that everyone who calls Georgia home has the freedom and opportunity to thrive—to live their very best lives!

"Vote for yourself. . . vote for the people you know and love, for the ones you work beside and worship with. For the Georgians you may never know but whose fate is undeniably tied to our own."

Our Chance. Our Choice. Georgia.

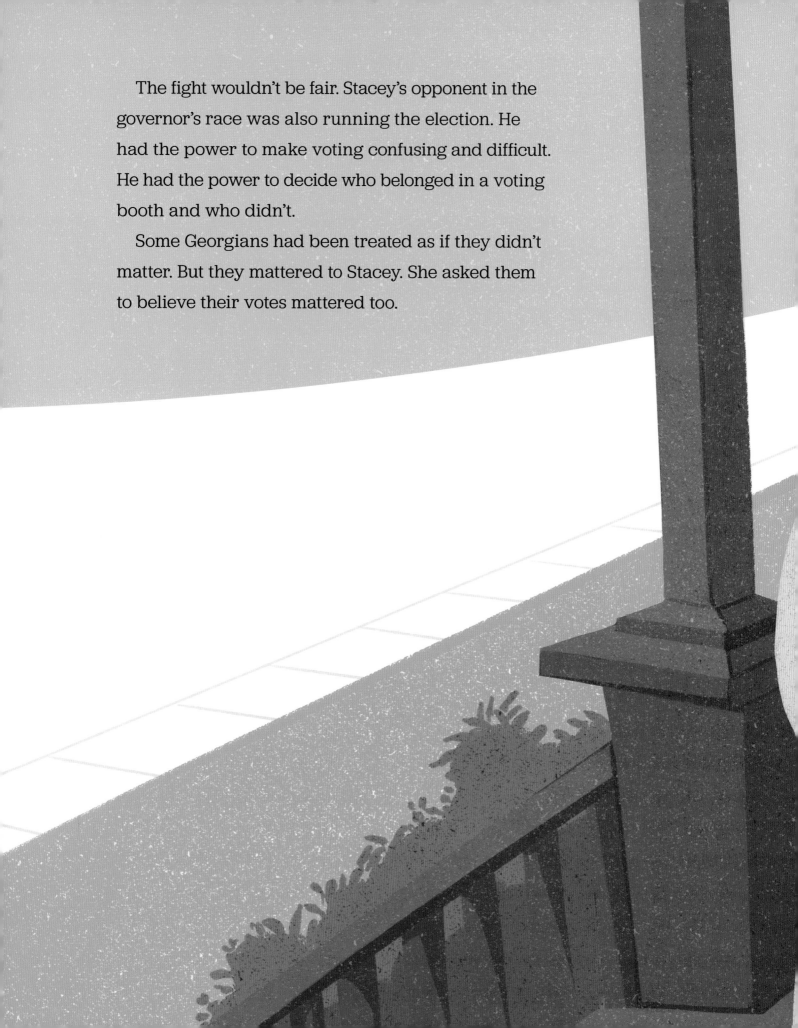

The fight wouldn't be fair. Stacey's opponent in the governor's race was also running the election. He had the power to make voting confusing and difficult. He had the power to decide who belonged in a voting booth and who didn't.

Some Georgians had been treated as if they didn't matter. But they mattered to Stacey. She asked them to believe their votes mattered too.

Election Day, 2018. Broken voting machines and too few polling places meant Black voters had to stand in line for hours. Names were missing from the lists of registered voters. Some Georgians didn't get real ballots at all.

Still, more voters than expected came out for the Georgia governor's election.

More Black voters.
More white voters.
More Asian voters.
More Latinx voters.
More young voters.

It wasn't enough.

Stacey wouldn't be in the governor's mansion. She let that fight go. She would lead from outside the gates.

"The title of governor isn't nearly as important as our shared title: Voters . . . I want to say thank you. Thank you to those of you who organized your communities and shattered records. . . . Change is not coming to Georgia. It has arrived. And you made it so."

Her parents had fought to make sure everyone was able to register, vote, and have their ballot count. Stacey would too.

She teamed up with other leaders to bring democracy to *all* the people. Workers across Georgia knocked on doors. They registered voters. They challenged unfair election rules. Across the country, people joined the fight.

In 2020, a pandemic closed schools, wiped out jobs, seized homes, and took loved ones. Now, more than ever, Stacey believed good leadership mattered. Another election was coming up. People deserved to have their voices heard and their votes counted.

Door to door, in phone call after phone call, volunteers asked: *Are you registered to vote? Do you know where to go? Are you sure?*

How can I help?

A Timeline of US Voting Laws— and Stacey Abrams

On February 12, 1900, Black students attending a segregated school gave a performance to commemorate Abraham Lincoln's birthday. They sang a new song with words written by their principal, James Weldon Johnson, and music by his brother, J. Rosamond Johnson. "Lift Every Voice and Sing" went on to become an anthem for Black Americans. The words celebrate Black life and Black history. They honor generations of mothers and fathers and kindred souls who triumphed over tyranny. Now, our voices join with theirs. The United States has come a long way. We still have a long way to go.

The Constitution of the United States promised that Americans would have a voice in their government. However, when the Constitution was approved by the states in 1788, many people living in the US were not considered citizens. Only white men who owned property could elect the officials who would represent their interests. In addition, each state established its own rules around voting, which often meant that someone's ability to vote was determined entirely by where they lived.

But people resisted. They demanded the right to participate in elections legally and safely. They fought for a true democracy. Over time, new laws, judicial rulings, and amendments to the Constitution have removed many barriers to voting, but individual states can still make rules that target particular groups and prevent some Americans from exercising their rights. Stacey Abrams and other civil rights leaders, community helpers, activists, and public servants work to give every eligible American the chance to vote. You can get involved. Ask questions. Learn about the voting rules in your area. Reach out to your leaders. Use your voice! How can you help?

1788 The United States ratifies its Constitution, which allows for the election of Representatives "by the People of the several States." In practice, most state-level laws exclude women, all non-white people, and white men who do not own land.

1843 Rhode Island drops its requirement that citizens must own property to be voters—one of the last states to do so. However, immigrants must still own land in order to vote.

1848 Under the Treaty of Guadalupe Hidalgo, people living in territories that Mexico lost to the United States in the Mexican-American War can choose to become US citizens.

1868 After the Civil War, the Fourteenth Amendment grants citizenship to everyone born or naturalized in the US, including all formerly enslaved people.

1870 The Fifteenth Amendment establishes that the right to vote shall not be denied on account of race. In response, some states pass laws or allow practices that make voting impossible for most Black Americans. Black voters are often physically attacked at the polls.

1920 The Nineteenth Amendment gives all women with US citizenship the right to vote.

1924 The Indian Citizenship Act extends citizenship to Native Americans. In response, some states pass laws to suppress Native American voting.

1943 The Chinese Exclusion Act ends, allowing people of Chinese descent to become citizens and vote.

1952 The Immigration and Nationality Act eliminates restrictions preventing people of Asian descent from becoming citizens.

1957 The Civil Rights Act of 1957 allows the federal government to investigate and stop voting discrimination. Civil rights leaders continue to organize marches and protests, fighting for the right to register and vote.

1964 The Twenty-Fourth Amendment prohibits the use of poll taxes in federal elections.

1965 **March 7:** Hundreds of peaceful civil rights protesters march in Selma, Alabama, as part of a Black voter registration drive. Police attack. People see television broadcasts of officers assaulting protesters. Outrage spreads across the country. More Americans join the fight for equality.

August 6: Driven in part by the public outcry for voter protections, President Lyndon B. Johnson signs the Voting Rights Act. States can no longer use unfair tests or other unfair laws to keep people from voting, and the federal government will supervise how elections are run in states that have previously violated the voting rights of their citizens. It takes years for some states to follow the law and protect all voters.

1971 The Twenty-Sixth Amendment lowers the voting age to eighteen.

1973 **December 9:** Stacey Abrams is born in Madison, Wisconsin, the second of six children born to Robert and Carolyn Abrams. The Abrams family later moves to Gulfport, Mississippi. Stacey grows up hearing stories of her parents' activism in the civil rights movement, such as her father's 1964 arrest for registering Black voters in Mississippi.

1975 Congress changes the Voting Rights Act to ensure that ballots and voting rules are offered in multiple languages.

1982 A bipartisan Congress and President Ronald Reagan renew the Voting Rights Act.

1984 The Voting Accessibility for the Elderly and Handicapped Act requires states to make sure that older Americans and Americans with disabilities have the space, technology, and support they need to cast their votes.

1989 The Abrams family moves to Georgia. Stacey is only in high school, but she gets a job working first as a typist and then as a speechwriter for a congressional campaign.

1991 Stacey graduates from high school and enrolls at Spelman College, a historically Black college for women in Atlanta, Georgia. She eventually serves as president of the Spelman Student Government Association.

1993 The National Voter Registration Act makes it easier for citizens to sign up to vote.

1995 Stacey graduates from Spelman College with top honors. She goes on to earn a Master of Public Affairs degree from the LBJ School of Public Affairs at the University of Texas and a law degree from Yale Law School. In her last year of law school, Stacey starts writing novels under the pseudonym Selena Montgomery.

1999 Stacey starts work as a tax attorney in Atlanta.

2002 The Help America Vote Act gives states basic guidelines for running fair elections.

2003 Stacey is appointed the Deputy City Attorney for Atlanta.

2005 Stacey launches a consulting firm—the first of several business ventures.

2006 Stacey is elected to the Georgia House of Representatives. She goes on to serve as the Georgia House Minority Leader—the first woman to lead in her state's legislature and the first Black woman to lead in the House of Representatives.

2013 In the case *Shelby County v. Holder*, the Supreme Court rules that states with a history of voter suppression no longer need to run changes to their election processes by the federal government, as the 1965 Voting Rights Act dictated, even if those changes make it harder for people to vote. States immediately begin enacting new restrictions that will primarily affect marginalized voters. In the years that follow, US senators and representatives propose many bills with new protections for voters, but they are not passed by Congress.

2013–2014 When Georgia's governor refuses to help the people in his state learn how to sign up for new national healthcare benefits, Stacey starts the New Georgia Project–Affordable Care Act, which hires Georgians to help their neighbors navigate the new healthcare system. Eventually the organization pivots to educating and registering new voters.

2018 Stacey becomes the Democratic nominee for governor of Georgia—the first Black woman to receive a gubernatorial nomination from a major party. Despite record turnout, Stacey does not have enough votes to be elected governor.

Voters in Florida pass Amendment 4 to restore voting rights to people charged with felonies once they carry out their sentences. In 2019, the state legislature passes a new law that blocks these voters until they pay any outstanding fees and fines.

2018–2019 Stacey starts a range of organizations to defend democracy and give Southerners the chance to thrive. One of them, Fair Fight Action, challenges voter suppression in court, pushes for legislation that will put a stop to unfair elections, and helps Georgians get the information and support they need to vote. Over the next two years, Fair Fight, the New Georgia Project, and other organizations register an estimated 800,000 new voters.

2019 Even though she no longer holds office, Stacey is chosen to give the Democratic Party's official response to the president's annual State of the Union address. She is the first Black woman to make this important speech.

2020 When the COVID-19 pandemic sweeps across the world, some states enact new ways for voters to participate safely in elections, particularly through early and mail-in voting.

2021 Stacey is nominated for a Nobel Peace Prize.

Georgia institutes new voting restrictions.

Stacey launches her second run for governor of Georgia.

Selected Bibliography

Abrams, Stacey. *Lead from the Outside*. New York: Henry Holt and Company, 2018.

———. *Our Time Is Now*. New York: Henry Holt and Company, 2020.

———. "Stacey Abrams in conversation with Alexis Madrigal." Interview with Alexis Madrigal. City Arts & Lectures, May 19, 2019. KQED broadcast, 1:11. https://www.cityarts.net/event/stacey-abrams/.

———. "Stacey Abrams, 'Lead From the Outside.'" Interview with Brooke Baldwin. Politics & Prose, April 9, 2019. Video, 49:49. https://www.youtube.com/watch?v=RLiSNUiMSvE&t=2039s.

Brennan Center for Justice. "Voting Rights Restoration Efforts in Florida." Brennancenter.org. Last updated September 11, 2020. https://www.brennancenter.org/our-work/research-reports/voting-rights-restoration-efforts-florida.

Downs, Jim, ed. *History in the Headlines: Voter Suppression in U.S. Elections*. Athens, GA: University of Georgia Press, 2020.

Garbus, Liz, and Lisa Cortés, dir. *All In: The Fight For Democracy*. Seattle, WA: Amazon Studios, 2020.

Lewis, John. "Why We Still Need the Voting Rights Act," *Washington Post*, February 24, 2013. https://www.washingtonpost.com/opinions/why-we-still-need-the-voting-rights-act/2013/02/24/a70a930c-7d43-11e2-9a75-dab0201670da_story.html.

Lyons, Kelly Starling. *Sing a Song: How "Lift Every Voice and Sing" Inspired Generations*. Illustrated by Keith Mallett. New York: Nancy Paulsen Books/Penguin Books for Young Readers, 2019.

Powell, Kevin. "The Power of Stacey Abrams," *Washington Post*, May 14, 2020. https://www.washingtonpost.com/magazine/2020/05/14/stacey-abrams-political-power/.

Rubin, Susan Goldman. *Give Us the Vote! Over 200 Years of Fighting for the Ballot*. New York: Holiday House, 2020.

Quotation Sources

p. 7: *"Go to church, go to school, and take care of each other."* Robert and Carolyn Abrams, as quoted by Stacey Abrams in her interview with Alexis Madrigal, City Arts & Lectures, May 19, 2019. KQED broadcast, 1:11. https://www.cityarts.net/event/stacey-abrams/.

p. 8: *"Having nothing is not an excuse for doing nothing."* Robert Abrams, as quoted by Stacey Abrams in "Watch Live: Oprah Campaigns with Georgia Democrat Stacey Abrams." *NBC News*. Streamed live on November 1, 2018. https://www.youtube.com/watch?v=oW9gL9nV8QI.

p. 8: *"Leadership . . . is about answering that question: How can I help?"* Stacey Abrams, in Kevin Powell's article "The Power of Stacey Abrams." *Washington Post*, May 14, 2020. https://www.washingtonpost.com/magazine/2020/05/14/stacey-abrams-political-power/.

p. 26: *"We are trying to create a state of excellent schools . . ."* Stacey Abrams, in a video included with Eugene Scott's article "Stacey Abrams's victory speech, annotated." *Washington Post*, May 23, 2018. https://www.washingtonpost.com/news/the-fix/wp/2018/05/23/stacey-abramss-historic-georgia-primary-victory-speech-annotated/.

p. 32: *"The title of governor isn't nearly as important as our shared title: Voters. . . ."* Stacey Abrams, in a video included with Gregory Krieg's article "Stacey Abrams says 'democracy failed' Georgia as she ends bid for governor." CNN, November 17, 2018. https://www.cnn.com/2018/11/16/politics/stacey-abrams-concession/index.html.

Visit SarahWBooks.com to see a recommended reading list and learn about other democracy champions.